A Monk
IN HIGH HEELS

living a cloistered life outside the monastery

Brenda A. Keller

ISBN: 147510684X
ISBN-13: 9781475106848

With loving gratitude to:

Meredith Gould, Ph.D. – for believing laughter and tears should exist together in good conversations; for loving God with me in the messy places; and for friendship unconditional, I'm eternally grateful.

The Rev. Tar Drazdowski – for being a gift to my life for a time such as this; for patiently answering questions and faithfully pointing to the Answer by counsel and example.

Thank you for being there and loving Him well. You inspire me.

Dedicated to:

The monks of the Abbey of Gethsemani,
The monks of the Monastery of the Holy Spirit,
and The real-world monks of The Virtual Abbey.
I'm grateful to be on the road Home to God with you.

The feeling remains that God is on this journey, too.

- ST. TERESA OF AVILA

Chapters

FORWARD....

I like this book.

𝕴 think the woman who wrote it is funny, honest, observant, and, best of all, does not take herself too seriously. All of which are very important qualities in a writer, especially one who writes about spiritual things. The alternative is to be dull, disingenuous, blind, and self-important which is what a lot of us who write about these things can be from time to time.

This is a book that can help open up a part of the Christian life that is largely unknown to much of the American Protestant community, a rich tradition that many have never been exposed to before. And having spent most of my life trying to do just such work myself, I think such work matters a lot.

I would also like to be as funny as she is for about twenty minutes before my life is done.

-Robert Benson, author of Between the Dreaming and the Coming True

Introduction

In essence, there is only one thing God asks of us — that we be men and women of prayer, people who live close to God, people for whom God is everything and for whom God is enough. That is the root of peace. — Brennan Manning

Stepping foot in a Trappist Monastery for the first time, I could hear the gentle rhythm of prayer echoing from a huge chapel as the wrought iron gate closed gently behind me. It was absolutely enchanting and one of those moments when I realized the soul was not just some abstract concept, but an actual place within me. I could easily have pointed to it and said, "God lives *here.*" Suddenly, my spiritual self came to life as if the melody escaping from the building had magnetically connected and refused to let go of anything and everything that mattered. I hadn't unpacked. I hadn't even checked in when I slid down the smooth wall of the chapel exterior and listened. I was mesmerized.

Too soon, the service ended and at least 35 monks clad in white and black robes emerged. I felt like I should move or get up or do something, but I just couldn't. Not yet. The monks all nodded in acknowledgement as they slowly walked by and not one looked at me as if he thought a girl in Capri pants and high heels should not be sitting next to a polka dot suitcase outside their holy chapel.

The wind picked up as I stood to my feet and I noticed for the first time the rolling hills and endless landscape. I'd never been one to pay enough attention to see God in nature, but I felt that shifting as I noticed the clouds descending to meet the horizon from somewhere many miles away. The trees were everywhere, one blending into the other, and it seemed every leaf was reaching toward heaven.

A few minutes later, I strolled to the guest house nearby to check in. One of the monks was already there sitting behind the desk reaching for his glasses while opening a big book of handwritten names near a rotary phone. Technology seemed a little lacking there and so far, no one acted like they were missing anything. He smiled as if, noticing me from a few moments earlier, we were already friends. He was warm, welcoming, and his soft eyes had a depth to them that far exceeded his age.

"Checking in?" He asked, snapping my wandering mind back to attention.

I nodded and my curiosity got the best of me. "What was...*that*?"

"*That*, my dear, was Vespers," he responded patiently.

"When does...*that*...happen again?"

"Tomorrow. Same time, same place, same thing, every day."

He didn't say it as if Vespers was a chore, or boring. He said it like it was the highest privilege ever afforded one on Earth. And in that moment I knew the secret to what my life was missing with God was right here, within these walls. All I had to do now was find it.

"We are all desperate, and that is, in fact, the only state appropriate to a human being who wants to know God."

— PHILLIP YANCEY

CHAPTER I

God within the walls

aking my key from the kind monk, I approached the retreat house feeling a little like an Amish woman might feel being dropped in the middle of Macy's against her will. My hair had been flat ironed into submission mere hours before, my clothes were modern and bright, and my shoes were high heel moderate adding three amazing inches to my otherwise limited verticalness. I'd never realized how much noise they made until they reverberated down the stone winding hallway and up every single step leading to my room. Although kind, people smiled with this strange knowing in their eyes and did look at me like they hoped that girl dressed for worldly success would find God within those walls. What they didn't know was that same girl was hoping more than anything for the very same thing.

Growing up in a Protestant tradition, I approached my first day at a Catholic monastery knowing less than nothing and feeling not just out of my element, but like I was doing something very wrong. I kept looking behind me expecting someone to tap me on the shoulder, lead me away and say, "You can't be here." Like a child at a local carnival hoping to ride the biggest roller coaster, I approached this experience certain that I wouldn't be tall enough to be there and not just physically. My whole life to that point was framed with the notion that "these people" of the Catholic tradition worshipped Mary, prayed to saints and did not know Jesus like I knew Jesus. I was encouraged to pray for them and whenever I encountered someone claiming to be Catholic, my heart sank just a little knowing they weren't "saved." That always sounded more like I found the magic ticket when they didn't and less like truth, but it was all I knew and what I carried with me that day. Not surprising then, when I turned the key, opening the squeaky door to my room in the guest quarters and the saw a huge cross with Jesus still on it, I freaked.

Several months before, a professor in college casually suggested in a seminar one day that everyone seriously seeking God needed a few days away for silence and prayer. She explained that in order to hear Him speaking, we would have to stop talking. That sounded reasonable enough. She described her time at a local monastery as serene and life changing and for whatever reason, I believed her. I'm not sure I'd even heard of a monastery before that day, but from that moment on, it consumed my every thought. I wondered what it would be like to be surrounded by that level of concentrated spirituality. I talked myself out of going at least twelve times a day. And for good reason. I was a student at a Methodist university. I didn't know anyone who claimed to be Catholic. It didn't make sense. But, I woke up in the morning thinking how much I needed a spiritual awakening and fell asleep knowing something had to change. Fresh life was going to be breathed into my stale relationship with the Almighty, or I wasn't going to make it.

Dealing with a minor depressive episode as a sophomore in college that should have been diagnosed a decade earlier was hard enough, but when the despair and hopelessness began seeping into my spiritual life, I knew I was in trouble. God had been more than just my stability; He had been my everything. And it scared me to death to go to sleep at night and listen to my soul ask the hard questions when answers were hard to find. Was God just a figment of my imagination? Was everything I had accepted as truth been a cruel lie of false hope and empty promises? God had been my closest and most consistent companion, but was He no more than the ultimate imaginary friend?

Tears streamed down my face night after night and soaked my pillow, but they were little consolation for questions without answers. Loneliness is a battle common to all in the human condition to varying degrees in different seasons, but spiritual loneliness is another animal all together. To approach the throne of grace and feel like no one's home is devastating. And feeling pretty certain the fault might be my own was neither comforting nor helpful. I would have done anything to make it better, yet could think of nothing.

I was desperate and didn't have the energy to argue denominational appropriateness. Perhaps it was that time in my life when I stopped caring how people categorized themselves religiously. It started to not mean very much to me whether one checked the box that said Lutheran, Catholic, Baptist, Church of Christ or Assemblies of God. I cared less about what people called themselves and more about what it meant for them to know God. What did a life of faith look like? How did one get from surface religion to a depth of spirituality that was sustaining? I had no idea. All I knew was I needed God where He could be found. And quickly.

I remembered the professor saying it took her months to get a reservation in the guest house. She mentioned openings were few and far between and that most people planned their visits a year or more in advance. Knowing this, one afternoon I worked up the courage to call hoping they would in fact not have an opening. Ever. The monk answering the phone spoke as if he had all the time in the world. It's a special gift to be able to make people feel like they are the only priority to another human, and he had that trait mastered. He was kind, patient, and I felt as if I could tell him anything and it would be absolutely okay. For the first time, the concept of confessing your sin to another person seemed completely reasonable. Not that I took that first encounter as an opportunity to unload my deepest, darkest secrets; only that I felt I could if I wanted to.

Taking the smallest leap of faith I could possibly muster, I mentioned my desire to come for a few days on a private spiritual retreat much later in the future, like never, and asked some general questions. I reminded him at least twice that I knew it would take a long time to get a reservation and I understood. I could hear him flipping pages before he asked enthusiastically, "How about Tuesday?"

"Tuesday? This Tuesday?" I asked anxiously.

He patiently replied, "Yes. This Tuesday. We don't usually have cancellations, but this one came up just before

5

you called and we have plenty of space for you." Remembering their vow of hospitality, I made a mental note to stop procrastinating immediately and stuttered, "Okay, but just for the day."

"We require a four day stay for any retreat, so how about coming on Tuesday morning and leaving late Friday evening? That should give you plenty of time to just be here with God," he suggested with a tone so welcoming I found myself agreeing. I thanked him and hung up the phone not sure what just happened. I didn't know where the monastery was, what happened in that holy place, whether I really belonged there, and more importantly, what I was supposed to wear.

In an act of great maturity, I did not call the professor and ask her every question I could think of to make my trip not only worthwhile, but without surprises. Even with limited knowledge, something deep within me suggested without a word that this experience was already bigger than I. This was a God thing and I had been around the spiritual block long enough to know that when God was up to something big, it was easier for both of us if I just let Him do the work. I'm a doer. I like to help, but I'm aware God doesn't always need my assistance or my opinion to accomplish his will. Sometimes He just needs my cooperation and more importantly, my surrender. So, from the time I said a little too enthusiastically, "Sure, Tuesday is great!" I genuinely surrendered.

Truth be told, I was already at the end of everything I knew about the spiritual life anyway. The God of my childhood who healed imaginary people on the flannel board was not putting the pieces together anymore. The Bible stories had been heard, explained, and acted out in Sunday school classrooms for a decade, but I couldn't find Him and I didn't know His role in my own story. I knew God was calling me deeper and into a more contemplative, mature relationship with Him even before I really knew what that meant. As with most spiritually significant moments, I can't entirely explain it. I can only say the winds of change were blowing and without question they were moving me to an experience that would make everything new.

For fear of looking spiritually weak, I didn't tell anyone what was going on and I never mentioned to a single friend I was headed to a monastery two hours away for a personal retreat. I was, after all, a psychology major and had no intention of using myself as a case study. Amazingly, no one even asked. Nothing electronic was allowed and the monk I spoke with suggested bringing very little to avoid worldly distractions. I'm the one who had a full scale panic attack when the airlines started charging for extra bags, so I'm always a bit nervous when people start throwing around the word minimal. I scanned my bookshelves, but none of the collections I depended on so frequently screamed at me to go along for the ride. I picked up a beautiful, leather bound embossed journal with my name in gold script that I had started six times in as many months. I noticed there was little more on the pages than the date and a simple, "Dear God, I can't find you." I chunked it in the nearby trash can.

I looked through my closet fairly certain that if I forgot something I wasn't going to be able to borrow a monk's habit or buy a girl cut t-shirt in the gift shop. I sorted through drawers wondering if jeans were appropriate or if I really needed church clothes. It was church, right? I had no idea. Finally, I packed what seemed sensible and comfortable and a whole lot of expectancy into a small suitcase. I walked out the door of that dorm room convinced, but not sure how, that when I returned through the same door nothing could ever be the same. What that would look like and how that would happen I wasn't sure. But, I was sure God was in this and I was His.

"Faith is what makes life bearable,
with all its tragedies and ambiguities
and sudden, startling joys."

— MADELEINE L'ENGLE

Chapter 2

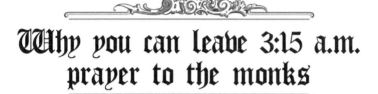

Why you can leave 3:15 a.m. prayer to the monks

Starting my first visit at the monastery without much preparation left me feeling, well, unprepared. Determined to get everything I could out of the four day commitment, I vowed to do as the monks did—no matter what. When they prayed, I would pray. When they read, I would read. When they ate (in silence!), I would eat whatever they did as quietly as I could. And when they spent time in reflection and meditation, I would *try*. Let's just say I tend to translate "be still and know" to "hurry up and go." All the time.

After checking in, unpacking, and changing into a pair of more appropriate flats, I returned to the lobby to have a chat with the nice monk at the front desk. I've never been anywhere else where hospitality is genuinely offered with no expectation of return kindness. It's not just the sign on the door, but an actual feeling that it is Christ himself who is doing the welcoming. I asked the monk for a printed schedule fairly certain there was not an app for that and he calmly replied, "Follow the bells."

I looked at him, confused. "Follow the bells, where?"

He really was the most patient man I'd ever encountered before and since. He managed to smile without being condescending and said, "The bells will lead you to prayer, dear. When they ring once, make your way to the chapel. When they ring twice, prayer begins. When they ring again, prayer has ended. The first prayer of the day is at 3:15 a.m. The rest of the day and night you will know to join us when you hear the bells. Just listen."

I instantly hoped the 3:15 a.m. bell was loud—really loud—and wondered if being awake before the Almighty was stirring wasn't a bit risky. Not feeling like I should argue with a man of God, I half smiled and said, perhaps a bit too enthusiastically, "See you there!" He laughed gently as if thinking this young woman in ironed linen pants and a tank top had no idea God was up to something big.

But, I saw it in the monk's eyes, he knew God had me on a spiritual quest, for a time such as this and he smiled in a way that made me want to know God like he did.

"Oh, and Brenda?" he asked quietly. "It's bedtime."

I looked up at the roman numerals of the huge clock behind his head. It was 7:45 p.m.

Longing to be just like the monks, I did go to my room, put on some comfy pajamas, crawled into the neat and simple twin bed with starched white sheets and a soft blanket and tried to sleep. There was no hum of a computer monitor, no dim light from an alarm clock or cell phone, and pretty much no noise at all. It was so, so, unbelievably quiet. Deafening. I quickly regretted the Venti Starbucks with an extra shot I'd had on the way over. I wanted to close my eyes and drift off into a blissful sleep in the most peaceful place on earth but, Jesus was staring at me from the wall and I was deathly afraid I would miss the bells. With no alarm clock, I feared that ignoring the first prayer of the day intentionally or not would surely end my career as monastic visitor of the year. I turned on the dim light beside the bed and paced the small room about seventy five times wondering how many people had walked that same floor and looked out the same sixth story window. I wondered how much business with God had been done in this 8x8 space of holy serenity. I pulled

13

aside the simple curtains and saw the grounds by stunning moonlight. The crosses from the nearby graveyard with small gold plates glistened and for the first time ever I felt not just surrounded, but comforted by such a great cloud of witnesses. I noticed the trees and the sidewalk and basked in the beauty of a place with exactly zero glitz or glamour. I realized the limited distractions imposed on those who entered here, that I found so constricting at first, were not only intentional, but vital.

Closing the curtains, I crossed my arms and leaned against the white painted walls. It bothered me, more than I thought it would, that not knowing a small thing like the time made me feel so out of control. I took deep breaths and tried to figure out what to do. I wasn't tired. I had nothing to keep me occupied. And just a few hours into the stay, my mind was still racing with the worries and concerns from life outside the monastery walls. I was alone with my thoughts and it was uncomfortable to say the least. Having tried everything else, naturally I attempted to be spiritual. I recited all the Bible verses I had committed to memory years earlier. That didn't really take very long. I tried to pray, but wasn't that the whole reason I was there? I couldn't hear from God and didn't have any idea what to say to Him anymore.

Finally, having worn myself out in every way, I sat on the floor and closed my eyes. I could feel the anxiety rising and even though I knew I was supposed to be there at that moment more than anywhere else in the world, I also wanted out. Immediately. What was I thinking? I couldn't spend four whole days at a monastery. I knew I had made a big mistake and ran through a plan to get home as soon as the sun came up. My soul was saying, "Be calm. You are here for a time such as this." But my brain was countering with, "May Day! May Day! Abandon ship!!"

When I opened my eyes post meltdown, I was staring straight at Jesus, still on the cross. I grew up in a tradition that rushed through the death of Christ to get to the joy and promise of the resurrection. I knew more about the Easter bunny than Lent and more about Saturday cartoons than Good Friday. I had no idea that people entered into a preparation period before Easter, but it seemed so right. I could almost feel my mind physically shift from the bloody mess of crucifixion to His gentle eyes that seemed to be staring straight into my soul. I already knew no one was around and even if there were I assumed judging people was frowned upon, so I looked up at him and out loud but quietly said in little more than a whisper, "Hi." I wouldn't say it was the peace that passes understanding necessarily, but it was peace none the less and it was jarringly recognizable having been missing for so long. I sat up slowly folding my hands wondering how long it had been since I'd taken the position of prayer and all of the sudden the floodgates opened. I had to tell Him everything.

The words came from somewhere deep within my soul at rapid fire pace. "I'm here because I can't find you anymore. I've loved you for 18 years, but now I'm not sure who you are, and more importantly, who you are to me. It's not enough to know the bible stories and recite the verses everyone knows anyway. I need to know You. I need you to not just matter to this life, I need you to *be* this life. I'm afraid and I'm lost without you. I'll do anything you say, everything you ask, and I'll surround myself with those who know you best until I can know you like that, too. And, someday, I'm going to want you to tell me how I'm even sitting here in this place, but that's not really important. I just want to know You now."

In that moment, I answered my own questions as to why God had led me gently and intentionally to that place, at that time, and I wept with soul cleansing gratitude. More than my next breath, I needed to find restored connection with my life source, my everything. I felt like my heart had started to beat and though the pulse was weak,

I was alive again. Convinced He was there, present and available, I knew I had to gather as much as I could and somehow get this experience home and into my real life. I wasn't sure how, but I had no other options. My very existence depended on it. I got up slowly, fell back onto the soft bed and fell asleep before my head hit the pillow.

I didn't have long to ponder my quest because just as I drifted off into the peaceful sleep I'd hoped for, I heard the bells beckoning me to Vigils, the first prayer office of the day. Led by the Spirit for sure I dressed quickly and walked the few feet to the main chapel pulling my hair up into a messy bun. Those who plan prayer at 3:15 a.m. cannot possibly expect visitors to look their best. I was actually thinking I should get a reward for not just hearing the bells, but showing up to prayer at all semi alert before coffee. Miracles really do abound in holy places.

> *Vigils: The office at night before dawn. A watch kept during normal sleeping hours.*
>
> No kidding.

I walked into the dark chapel with candles burning and monks slowly processing. They looked much more alert than I felt like, perhaps, they had been on this schedule for a few decades or more. I watched their faces of quiet expectancy and felt my soul quicken. God was not just at this monastery in some generalized He is everywhere kind of way. God was *there* in that room right then. The monks came to the aisle and one by one bowed in the Cistercian tradition of a deep bow with the hands together near the knees. I didn't know at that time they were reverencing the reserved sacrament, but I could almost feel from their simple bow they were saying to God, "I'm here. You're here. That's enough." I still think about that day every single time I approach the altar at my own church.

As beautiful as that moment was, there was no denying. It was early. And dark. And I was suddenly glad I remembered someone saying the night before that praying any particular hour of prayer did not, in fact, take a whole hour. Everyone sat in complete silence, the monks in their wooden seats separated by the main isle and facing one another. The layout of most monastic chapels is designed so that one faces their brothers straight on. There is no worshipping God alone at the hours of prayer. He is worshipped in community. The retreat guests were seated in the area next to them secluded yet a part. I couldn't even hear anyone breathing. The ADD part of me wanted to jump up and shout, "What are we waiting for? I'm falling asleep here. Let's go!! Pray!" but that seemed not good so I refrained. Then, awakening me from my thoughts, a bell rang. Of course. "Ding. Ding." It was simple, but so profound that I felt the reverberations deep within my soul. I could not remember another moment in my entire life that I was that in tune with the Almighty. In that corporate setting, in that beautiful chapel, in that hard wooden seat in the middle of complete strangers, God and I were one.

In a monastery setting 3:15 a.m. or any time really is fine for prayer. There's not much else to do and the whole reason people go is to reconnect on a spiritual level. It's easy to get caught up in the rhythm of the predictable schedule and peaceful culture. Getting up at 3 a.m. is not so hard when you call it a day at 8 p.m. But, the monastery is not the real world to be sure. In everyday life there are multiplied distractions and they are increasing for most of us daily.

I vowed leaving the monastery the first time that I would continue on with a life of prayer similar to the monks. I would set my alarm and get up to spend a few quiet moments with God every single day. And I would keep the rest of the prayer schedule too. I was determined to make a way to be like them in the real world. I wasn't home ten minutes before I knew that was an impossibility to say the least. I had other responsibilities and pausing to pray at a certain time every day without fail was not only inconvenient for me, but often for those around me.

Ironically, twelve years later, I do get up most mornings at 3:15 a.m. without an alarm clock for prayer not because I have to, but because I want to. I find the time of day when it isn't quite morning and it's not really night a thin place where God is closer than a whisper. It's the perfect opportunity for this life to reflect on the day before and embrace the hours to come. And if that's a good time for prayer for whatever reason, do it. But, if it isn't, and it probably won't be, start the day with prayer whenever the day begins. 7 a.m. 8 a.m. 9 a.m. or noon. The important part is pausing to pray, dedicating the day ahead and beginning with an intentional effort to connect with God. For most people, this means leaving 3:15 a.m. prayer – to the monks.

Almighty God, to you all hearts
are open, all desires known, and
from you no secrets are hid: Cleanse
the thoughts of our hearts by the
inspiration of Your Holy Spirit,
that we may perfectly love you, and
worthily magnify your holy Name;
through Christ our Lord. Amen.

— THE COLLECT FOR PURITY, BCP 1979

CHAPTER 3

Meditation. Not the same as sleep.

As if getting up in the middle of the night for prayer wasn't spiritual enough, immediately following the office of Vigils is forty five minutes of silent prayer and meditation in the chapel. That sounded like such a good idea in theory, but I'm not going to lie, I was nervous. Sit in the dark staring at nothing but darkness for almost an hour "meditating"? I had failed multiple times at home to meditate for even three minutes straight without making a grocery list in my head. My best time ever may have been about two solid minutes and that was on cold medicine. This was not good, but it was also way too late.

The other retreat visitors beside me were brilliant. They pulled the Protestant card and snuck out during the final moments of the prayer service. So, even better, I was alone in complete stillness and couldn't get up without opening and closing an ancient door that squeaked. Fantastic. I folded my hands hoping that even if I couldn't pull off the whole seriously meditating thing, I could at least look the part. The chair wasn't comfortable and it was ridiculously cold in there. I realized quickly that may have been on purpose. All that was actually missing to make this experience quite possible and maybe even enjoyable was a Starbucks. I shook myself awake from my caffeine dreams, rubbed my tired eyes red from crying the night before and made an intentional effort to focus.

I gave myself a little pep talk. "You can do this! You. Are. Spiritual! Just yesterday you weren't talking to God, and today you are praying with monks! What a difference a day makes!" I halfway believed myself.

From seemingly nowhere Psalm 23 popped into my mind as if the Almighty wanted to keep me occupied as much as I didn't want to embarrass myself by falling asleep on the waxed floor beneath me. The words were so

familiar and yet brand new. I heard every one for the first
time as they dropped into my subconscious.

The LORD is my shepherd,
I shall not want.
He makes me lie down in green pastures;
He leads me beside quiet waters.
He restores my soul;
He guides me in the paths of righteousness
For His name's sake.

He restores my soul. He restores my soul. He restores
my soul, began to echo from that place where God lives.
It slowed to a snail pace. He. Breathe. Restores. Breathe.
My. Breathe. Soul. Quickly the simple words I had known
for a lifetime turned into the first prayer my heart had truly
prayed in months. Energized by the Holy Spirit's presence
in a moment where peace wraps around a heart like a well
worn blanket comfortable and familiar, I relaxed into the
hard chair that begged for perfect posture.

The words began to change as they repeated.

You restore my soul. *You* restore my soul. *You* restore
my soul.

By the time I found myself in that moment, I had loved
God for most of my life. He had always made sense to

me. Love God, always have company and avoid Hell? Yes, please. I sat on a couch as a seven year old and "accepted Christ as my Savior" like I had been told to by those who loved me most. And I believed then and still do that God moved from an abstract concept of my young life, into the forefront of everything at that moment. I was all in. Well, as much as a seven year old can be all in.

I didn't yet have the maturity to know that a relationship with God is ever evolving. I didn't know that as age and experiences presented themselves, I would relate to God differently. And I didn't understand that I would meet Him at the intersection of grace and mercy throughout my life including that day. I would know Him differently from that moment on, but I knew in all the ways that mattered He would be the same. He was still so faithful to me, a human. There wasn't a monumental sin that separated me from the Almighty in my college years. I certainly hadn't decided to leave Him along the side of the road as my life advanced and my priorities changed. Nonetheless, we had grown apart and I had the sinking suspicion that He was still where He had always been. The problem was me.

Tears were streaming down my face in that chapel amidst a holy moment of transcendence. Everything else became irrelevant and the line between heaven and earth was pleasantly blurry at best. I took comfort in the rows of tissue neatly placed under every seat. Tears were welcome here. Expected even. When I looked up, the monks had left and I was alone in the solitude and silence. I felt small, but safe. Insignificant, but loved. I didn't know how long I'd been sitting there alone or how much time had passed. And it didn't matter at all. I couldn't be sure, but it felt strangely like meditation had just happened without much effort on my part. And maybe that was the secret.

I had always thought of meditation as a bald Buddah guy sitting cross legged on the floor of an Ashram humming some sound until he was liberated to an out of body experience of complete and total zen. I knew the scriptures spoke of meditation, but as to what that meant or how it could be accomplished, I was clueless. I found great peace in discovering that meditation could be a single word, phrase, or verse or nothing at all depending on the season where I found myself wading through. Meditation for hours on end in complete silence was never going to work with my personality. I could experience it in other ways that worked with how I operated and still find God in those places. And even though over the years my meditation practice has gotten more focused and enjoyable, I still wouldn't say it was my spiritual gift.

Later that same day at the monastery I walked the path of a labyrinth around and around in concentric circles until I reached the middle. I said a prayer and then returned in a circular pattern back to the place where I began. I emptied my mind of the stress and fear through the process. I exited the labyrinth feeling much lighter, freer and very similar to what I'd experienced in the chapel that morning. Later a friend would explain that moving meditation is not only easier for some people, but often the only way they can participate in this ancient practice. Movement to find stillness? Strange but true.

I have experienced meditation differently over the years. Sometimes in a quiet room with a single candle I will discover that still small voice within me that begs to connect with something greater than myself. Other times I find the perfect prayer in my yoga practice with the movement and breathing centering my mind. I'm pretty sure in a Christian mindset we either make meditation into some weird new age creepiness or so difficult that no one can master it. And that last part might be true. Meditation, like everything else that matters most, is a practice. Setting a clock for a certain amount of time or insisting on participating in the same way as everyone else is unlikely to produce the desired outcomes of calm and peace. What works for you may not work for me and vice versa. And that's okay. The important thing is to create a space for it, adjust it when necessary and come without

expectations. Be open. Be present. Be willing to be inter-
rupted. And be patient with yourself when it takes longer
than expected to find the peace you crave. It's not easy and
often times almost impossible to completely remove the
pressures and concerns of this world from a busy mind.
But, I think God understands and is not surprised by that.
Jesus lived among those who came before us, and even
though he didn't have an iPhone, he was accustomed to
distractions. We can plan, prepare, and create the perfect
atmosphere according to what we think is best, but He
tends to fill in the blanks with results far greater than we
could anticipate anyway when we give our time to Him.
And usually it's enough to just show up.

"In solitude we realize that nothing human is alien to us."

— HENRI NOUWEN

CHAPTER 4

Lectio Divina — Divine Reading

Occasionally I operate on the assumption that more at a faster pace is best. Okay, all the time. I like to accomplish a lot in an order that makes sense to me and to cross the finish line of my own making victoriously and preferably ahead of schedule. And that works okay when it comes to cleaning the house, finishing a novel, or running a marathon. It doesn't seem to be very effective when the goal is to develop a deeper spiritual understanding of God and the scriptures.

Several years ago a major Bible publisher introduced a 90 day Bible to the market broken into pieces where one could read the entire scripture in three months. The whole thing. It sounded like a challenge I had to take and not just because if it was finished in time there would be a championship (??) t-shirt in the mail. Read the whole Word of God in such a short time? I expected awesome spiritual results along with a triumphant victory. And maybe some bragging rights. I mean great humility. And I did read all of it in the allotted time, but I got absolutely nothing beneficial from it. Nada. I had to read at a rapid fire pace and found myself just getting through the reading for the day instead of focusing on the words coming from the ancient pages. It was simultaneously a success and an epic failure. Every time I wear that t-shirt today I still think, "Wow, that was totally pointless."

It was at the monastery that I was first introduced to the idea of Lectio Divina or divine reading. Once practiced by all Christians, the tradition is primarily kept alive today in the hearts of true monastics. Along with the Liturgy and daily work, lectio divina offers the final piece of a balanced life to maintain spiritual rhythm. It can be practiced in various ways by individuals or groups, but it becomes an art form where simplicity and connectivity is developed through the slow and purposeful reading of the holy scriptures. Any passage, verse, book or even word is appropriate for this practice, but it is recommended that a shorter portion is chosen especially at the beginning. The goal is never quantity.

Scheduled into the daily life of a monk is Lectio Divina. Guigo, a 12th century Carthusian monk described this practice in several stages that are still used today. The first stage is lectio or reading. Slowly and reflectively the word of God is read until it sinks deep within our being. This can be out loud or silently, but is typically done in the monk's chambers alone. St. Benedict in the Prologue to the Rule recommends that people learn to "listen with the ear of our hearts." These initial moments involve an aspect of quieting down, slowing the mind, and embracing the stillness. Instead of reading for quantity, we are participating in reverential listening for sole purpose of intimate connection with God through His word.

O God, You are my God; I shall seek You earnestly;
My soul thirsts for You, my flesh yearns for You,
In a dry and weary land where there is no water.
Thus I have seen You in the sanctuary,
To see Your power and Your glory.
Because Your loving kindness is better than life,
My lips will praise You.
Psalm 63

The second stage is meditatio or reflection. A reader pauses from the passage of scripture and considers what they've read. What does it mean? And more importantly, what does it mean – to them? We consider what God might be saying within those words and how they can be applied to a modern day setting. We learn, as the Virgin Mary did, to ponder these words in our heart (Luke 2:19). They become more than His words. They become His words – for us. And in that moment, scripture takes on a more personalized meaning for the life participating in the practice.

How does living in a sanctuary help to see Him? Power and glory is there, but how do I see it? God treats me with love and kindness always, so what should my response be to others I encounter today?

The third stage is oratio or prayer/response. At this stage we leave our thinking behind and let our hearts say what they will to God. This develops from the reflection on the reading and we return God's words to Him in the way we understand them. There is no right or wrong way. We understand prayer as a loving dialogue with God who has invited us to be in communion with Him. We allow this relationship with the One who knows us best, to change us from the deepest core of our beings. We bring our hardest, and most painful moments to the surface and vulnerably open our hearts enough to allow

God to bathe those things in His infinite love and healing grace. Although it sounds so wonderfully cleansing, it is not easy. There is no such thing as independently mastering surrender. We have to let go. It helps me at times to open my hands to Him, turn them over and say, "God. I've emptied me of me. Fill me with you."

You are my God. The most important thing to me. I do long for You, your company, your presence. Even in the times when I cannot find you, you are there. I give you praise because you are my everything and more important than my next breath. I give you the parts of me that resemble you and those that hurt your image and damage your reputation and ask you to make me like you. Only you.

The last stage is contemplatio or contemplation/rest. This is perhaps the hardest part of the practice. We find words to be unnecessary and that they cannot adequately describe the experience we've had in the presence of Christ anyway. We have to just be. We lay aside our reading, our evaluating, our words and even our intentions and we make ourselves available for God to show up in whatever way He chooses. When we've done the work of the previous stages, we will experience the unmatched joy of just being in the presence of God. Like sitting on the back porch with a friend on a breezy Saturday afternoon and without saying a word feeling like we've had the best conversation of our lives.

We have to be willing to sacrifice all manner of being goal oriented. There is no goal in lectio divina except spending time with God through His word. Period. There's no other way to do it. There are no shortcuts. We participate by reading, reflecting, and releasing over and over again day after day for a lifetime. People from ancient days described an inner spiritual forward motion as a helix or an ascending spiral. In the studying and then giving of ourselves to God, we are drawn closer to Him as we cover ascending ground closer and closer to His heart. Spiritual activity and receptivity circle us closer to our real core back and forth, or in the words of C.S. Lewis' Narnia, "Further up and further in." It's not reading just to read. It's not putting time in and checking off a box just to say we've done it. Lectio Divina is slowing down and consuming scripture in a way that when we close the book and get up from the desk, having been bathed and renewed by the unmatched presence of God himself, we are never the same.

Bringing Lectio Divina home

Lectio Divina, even in a monastic setting, is done privately. This makes it fairly easy to take home and apply it to a more normal life. Choose a text of scripture of interest. Some use a portion of the Eucharistic liturgy and others work slowly through a book of the Bible. It honestly makes no difference at all. Find a comfortable spot and take a few moments to become as still as possible. More often than not, before I enter into Lectio Divina, I intentionally breathe in love, strength and peace and breathe out fear, anxiety, and stress. At times, once through that exercise is plenty. There have been many others when thirty minutes later, I'm still trying to breathe in love never getting to strength and peace. And that's okay. These words are interchangeable depending on the season, situation and need. Find what works for you and do it. Make a habit of it until it becomes a practice your soul craves. Then allow yourself to be changed by it.

Approach the text you've chosen slowly and with much grace. Leave your expectations elsewhere. Listen for the still, small voice. Then take what you've read into your heart. Do not be afraid of memories or thoughts that surface. These are part of the experience. Give them to God and allow Him to work. Use words to express to Him the feelings as they arise. And when you've said what needs emptying from your heart, rest. Learn the difference between using words and letting them go when they are no longer needed.

Listening and being led by the Holy Spirit is a lifelong process and one that won't be mastered in a short time of prayer. You may return to the text many times during this practice or once may be enough. A single word or phrase may stand out as particularly applicable that day and you can take it from there into the experiences you are having. The Word of God is only still alive when it is alive in you. And in that moment, Lectio Divina gets lived out in it's purest form. It changes you from the inside and affects the outside.

People long for that ancient connection to God, especially in an age of increased conflict and crisis. Knowing that many others have encountered God in this way should be encouraging. By reuniting with Christ through Lectio Divina on a regular basis, ideally daily, we discover that same spiritual rhythm that maintained many who have come before us. It becomes the driving force of our lives. Spiritual activity and receptivity become constant companions. And anytime throughout the day we can connect with that ascending helix once again and remember we're on the way Home to Him. He invites us to let him join our journey by our surrender.

Lectio Divina teaches us that God loves us. We come to remember that even as we desire to find His heart, he is ever reaching for ours. And that embrace is real. We feel God's love and we know that we can be changed by that same love. And this practice teaches us about ourselves. We learn that there is no hidden corner of our hearts, no unturned stone that God is not willing and able to uncover and heal. All of what we have been, all of what we are currently, and all of what we hope to become gets handed over to the One whose plan is perfect. The eternal map maker whispers in our ears, "I know the way. I am the way. And I will lead you home." We surrender our agenda and learn to trust through the daily and willing surrender of a longing heart in tune with Him.

It doesn't interest me where, or what,
or with whom you have studied.
I want to know what sustains
you from the inside when all else
falls away.

— Oriah Mountain Dream

CHAPTER 5

Labor as an act of love

It's easy to think of the monastic life as a somewhat relaxed existence. Like a beautiful church service that never ends. Companionship with like minded believers in a place where ancient traditions are soaked into every brick. A scheduled spiritual life that's only invitation is to follow. Prayer followed by reading then work followed by meals followed by more prayer over and over again day after day. And there's no denying it, a lot of prayers are offered up in a twenty four hour period at any monastery. But, that's not the whole of the lives of those who live within the walls. Being cloistered is to be set apart by definition and reality. For the spiritual retreat attendee, the monastery is a spiritual oasis, but it's important to

41

remember that these beautiful structures are also their homes. They eat there, work there, sleep there, have medical care mostly there and have church there. They don't have their own transportation and rarely leave. Some may take extended leave due to illness, visit family members, or spend time at another abbey. But, for most of their lives, they are there. And they know what they're getting into when they sign on. One of the most respectable aspects of the setup of the monastic community is their ability to remain self-sufficient. They in no way live lavishly, but their needs are provided for without government assistance and they help to contribute to their own needs by the work they do.

For the Abbey of Gethsemani in Kentucky, it's an entire operation of cake and fudge making that is distributed throughout the country especially at the holidays. For the Monastery of the Holy Spirit in Conyers, GA, their financial needs are met by fruitcake, fudge, coffee grown by the monks and honey from bees on their grounds. And for the Abbey of New Mellary in Iowa, their lifestyle and ministry are supported by caskets and urns handmade and shipped for services all around the world to minister to people in their time of grief.

Abbeys take the reminder from scripture that those who don't work, don't eat quite seriously. Every monk who is physically able is assigned a specific duty according to their gifts and talents. During work periods, monks are seen tending to the garden that provides much of the food for the abbey. Other brothers are cleaning or cooking. Many participate in whatever the specialty is at that specific monastery in every aspect from ordering supplies to creating the product to shipping the finished masterpiece.

I watched several of the monks one afternoon from the bench in the middle of the courtyard where I was reading quietly. One was weeding the garden. One was sweeping the sidewalk. Another was carrying paint cans to an area outside my vantage point. They moved methodically, purposefully. Occasionally they would say something to the other monks near them, but mostly they worked like caring for the property entrusted to them was not just important to their survival, but part of their calling.

After watching them for a few moments I realized why I was so fascinated with what they were doing. They not only made work a priority, they made it an act of prayer. Their faces were calm and intentional. I heard no complaining or talk of wishing their duties could be different. I doubt any of them as a seven year old boy when the neighbor who asked what he wanted to be when he grew up, responded, "the guy who chops carrots in the monastery kitchen." But, that is where the short monk with the deep smile lines and thick glasses found himself at sixty five years of age and honestly, he seemed happier in his work than I did in mine. It didn't appear to make a difference what any of them were doing, it was the attitude with which they approached all things. Like it mattered. Like they could see the bigger picture. Like they knew they were a small piece in a greater puzzle that would outlast their earthly existence. Removing a weed seemed insignificant to me especially spiritually, but in that small way, they were making the world a better place. They were maintaining not just a physical home, but a spiritual one that would nourish and strengthen men to come after them that maybe weren't even born yet. They worked unto God and it showed.

And I wondered how I could take that home, into my work and into my life. Sure, maintaining monastery grounds could be seen as purposeful work in such a spiritual setting fairly easily. But, what about those who punch a clock and pray for 5:00 like their lives depend upon it? What about the people who feel their work is insignificant and the pay checks barely provide enough food to care for them and their families? And what about the millions of people without work in a failing economy who have lost everything? Unfortunately, I don't have all those answers. And I understand that it's far easier for those who live within the walls and do the duties they're assigned without fear of unemployment. A lot of worldly cares are absent from the monastery by nature of the environment they call home.

I don't know the work God has called you to or the duties he's assigned that require your participation while you spend time on this Earth. It's likely not the same plan He has for my life. And I don't know how you feel about His plan for you, whether you like your gifts and talents or whether you feel like you're contributing to society in a positive way at all. But, stay with it. Keep asking Him. Keep looking for either new opportunities, or for new eyes to see how the current ones matter. The guy pulling the weeds in the garden make the life easier of the monk harvesting the carrots. The monk cleaning and cutting the carrot makes the monk's job cooking the soup much faster. And the soup brought to the table by the serving monk has really just completed the task of the monk pulling the weeds. It's the cycle of life. Working as unto the Lord might mean you get to be part of the finished product sometimes. But, more often than not, you'll be somewhere in the process trusting for greater results.

People who pray, really pray, do not talk about it much.

— EMILIE GRIFFIN

CHAPTER 6

Kindness to God

Often in a monastic setting, spiritual guidance is offered in the form of various retreats or private sessions. These several day getaways may cover specific topics such as prayer or living a contemplative life. A local monastery has a three day retreat that focuses on yoga as prayer that I attended last year. It was transformative on so many levels and I was able to do the work in three days that I could not accomplish on my own at home after months of trying. Gentle guidance with like-minded people in a peaceful setting was the climate I needed for serious change. I'm forever grateful.

Upon entering a monastery several years ago, I walked past the monk sitting at the front desk calmly staring into space. This was my first visit to this place and so I stopped by his desk to pick up a map and schedule. He greeted me warmly and asked, "Do you require spiritual assistance during your stay with us?"

I had come with my own agenda, my own work to do, my own reading material and my own plans, but I thought it was nice of him to ask. "No thank you."

He smiled, "Then may you find the answers you seek in God alone."

Those words have never left me.

On that particular trip they were offering a walk with a monk to discuss an unannounced spiritual principle and, needing the exercise, I decided to go along. As it turned out, I was the only one who wanted to walk in the 90 degree August heat on a path with no shade with a habit clad monk in simple sandals. "Ready?" I nodded and followed him into the blazing sun and into the heart of God.

We walked at least a mile before he said anything. My focus was on not tripping and falling on the rugged terrain and trying not to sweat to death wondering why neither of us thought water was a good idea. He seemed unfazed by the blazing sun and dry air. I turned my weary head toward him as I heard him say, "Kindness."

Unable to stop myself and a touch irritable by the conditions, I asked, "Kindness, what?"

Wisely, he said nothing and continued to walk one foot in front of the other. I rolled my eyes immediately thankful we were both looking straight ahead. I didn't know the grounds well enough to know whether we were walking in a loop, or a hundred miles out just to turn around and walk a hundred miles back. I couldn't help but think, "In my feeble attempt to try to live like a monk, I'm going to die like one right here on the monasatic grounds."

"Kindness," he stated again slowly. I'm sure he picked up on my increasing attitude, but he didn't allow my behavior to affect his. Bummer. "Let's talk about kindness, shall we?"

"Sure, why not?" I asked with about as much enthusiasm as an appointment for a root canal. We walked another half mile and I realized this conversation was going to take the rest of my life to finish. I had fallen behind him just a few feet and when he stopped I came about a millisecond away from running smack into him. He sat on a bench that I hadn't even noticed was there and gently patted the spot next to him. I sat down worn out in every way. We stared into the vast openness of the land in front of us and for the first time I noticed how beautiful it was. Breathtaking, really. I could feel my heart rate slowing and my breathing quickly followed.

I had almost forgotten the monk was there when I heard him ask quietly, "Are you kind to yourself?" My defenses started to rise, but I didn't have the energy to translate that into coherent sentences. Following the monk's wise example, I said nothing for awhile and waited for the words to come. He waited too, comfortable enough to not fill in the silence with words. I couldn't put on false pretenses, and it suddenly didn't matter to me if this man of God thought I was sufficiently spiritual or the worst human being to ever walk the face of the earth. I just wanted more than anything to be in that moment and to be more honest than I'd ever been.

"Kind to myself," I repeated carefully considering my answer. "No, not really. No, not at all." I wasn't even sure what I meant by that, but I knew it was the truth. He nodded slowly as if that was the answer he was expecting. I paused awaiting a great spiritual answer and explanation that would forever make me a holier Christian and a better human being.

Naturally, he said nothing. At all. Not even anything to make me feel better about my faulty humanity. I sat there alone with my thoughts and he, well, sat there. After about 20 minutes, no kidding, he emerged from the silent abyss and asked, "Are you kind to others?" I knew the answer right away, but I waited because that seemed fair. If he wasn't going to answer me in a timely fashion,

I wouldn't answer him either. So there. Feeling like I'd waited long enough, I replied, "No. Not like I should be." Again, he nodded with the wisdom of one content to ask the questions without knowledge of the answers. By then I didn't expect him to answer and he did not.

Another little while passed before he asked the third and final question. "Would you say you are kind to God?" Having finally been given the opportunity to discuss, I couldn't find a single word to say. I had never considered kindness to God. I knew He was kind to me when he answered my prayers in the way I requested within the time frame I suggested. I knew I viewed Him as unkind when I didn't get my way and couldn't find him in present uncomfortable and often seemingly unfair circumstances. I wordlessly realized in that moment that God's kindness to me had until that point been dependent on my perception and not his unchanging character.

"Are you kind to God?" he asked patiently.

I answered honestly, "I don't know. Maybe sometimes. Maybe not. I've never thought about it before, but my preliminary answer would have to be no. I'm demanding and impatient. His love is unconditional and his mercy infinite, but I offer myself to him with unfair limitations and questionable expectations all the time." I took a deep discouraged breath and sighed. I felt like such a bad person and an ungrateful child of the most high.

He stood without saying a word and began to walk slowly back to the main monastery. I followed him for over a mile lost in my own thoughts and spiritual defeat. He stopped atop a hill where we could see how far we'd come and our destination simultaneously. He crossed his arms and shuffled his feet in the sandy soil beneath him. When he looked up, for the first time he locked eyes with me in a way that suggested this was going to be important. "God understands," he said as if that was the answer to everything. "God understands." He turned on his heels and led me back to the monastery where we parted ways without another word. I slowly climbed the stairs back to my room and fell to my knees beside my small twin bed needing a conversation with God more than a shower. I found my normally rambling self without much to say.

I laid my head on the worn quilt and rested in the arms of the Almighty before I quietly whispered, "I'm so sorry." In only four questions the monk had pointed me to the Answer. "God, make me kind. To others. To myself. And to You."

Never had another human being in so few words broken my heart and restored it again with the presence of the Healer.

"Every Christian needs a half-hour of prayer each day, except when he is busy, then he needs an hour."

— Francis de Sales

CHAPTER 7

The Divine Office

There's something so comforting about spending a day or two with prayer as the primary and only focus. After a little while, the anxiety and overwhelmed silence that initially seemed so foreign and uncomfortable gets replaced by quiet joy and surrender. I always know I've reached that place of spiritual peace when, on the second or third day of my monastic retreat, the thought enters my mind. "I was made for this." The creator is as easy to find as my own heartbeat. Easier maybe. At last I can breathe again. The strained lines have disappeared from my forehead and my eyes look rested without $40 worth of retinol. I've stopped wondering if the universe quit revolving as soon as my iPhone got turned off and placed in a lock box in an office somewhere. I start to feel like myself, how I'm made to be. No stress. No pressure. No agenda except to reconnect with God. Starting the day with prayer and ending it in the same way is a privilege and I appreciate those set apart times I've experienced to recharge spiritually. God is everywhere and always available in a standard spiritual setting or an ordinary one for sure, but checking in at the chapel seven times a day provides a peaceful structure unmatched elsewhere.

The hours of prayer are nothing new. The Greeks, Jews, and Romans separated the time between sunup and sundown into twelve parts, many of which the Jews devoted to prayer.

Now, when Daniel knew this, that is to say, that the law was made, he went into his house: and opening the windows in his upper chamber towards Jerusalem, he knelt down three times a day, and adored and gave thanks before his God, as he had been accustomed to do before. Daniel 6:10

The Apostles continued the Old Testament condition. *Now Peter and John went up into the temple at the ninth hour of prayer. Acts 3:1*

Early Christians carried on this tradition which eventually developed into the canonical hours, or offices of prayer eventually known as The Divine Office. The times and schedules for different monasteries vary as do the prayers themselves, but typically they follow a similar pattern.

3:15 a.m. Vigils – The night office

5:45 a.m. Lauds – Morning Prayer

6:15 a.m. Eucharist

7:30 a.m. Terse

12:15 p.m. Sext

2:15 p.m. None (rhymes with bone)

5:30 p.m. Vespers – Evening Prayer or Evensong

7:30 p.m. Compline – Night Prayer

I visited several monasteries in the decade following my first moments there. Usually during a season where I needed God to show up, I would escape for a few days to mend a broken heart, restore a soul, seek answers or find Him to be faithful once again. I always felt connected to the prayers wherever I was even though they differ slightly from one community to another. From the watching area of the visitor seats and occasionally in the stalls with the monks themselves, I found God in the ancient traditions and rhythms of prayer over and over again. My faith grew and my love for Him developed in those divine offices. The liturgical tradition connected to this soul in ways I had yet to understand. But, the spark was there and when I really needed to find God, when I really needed to hear

Him call my name and listen for His heartbeat, I could feel it grow brighter and call me into His presence with those who love Him most consistently.

After visits to monasteries near and far, I returned to the Protestant tradition for a solid decade. It was comfortable. It was what I knew, but over the years it grew less and less fulfilling. I missed the liturgy. I missed the reverence. My soul felt incomplete, but I had no idea where to find that sacred connection in the real world. I believed those monastic prayers existed within the walls of an abbey and not in my real life with "regular" people. And I sat in pews Sunday after Sunday, week after week, month after month and year after year getting fed spiritually for sure, but missing that sacred connection. At times it was unnoticeable, but during other seasons the flame threatened to take me over. I grew frustrated with my spiritual life and felt as if I'd come full circle only to discover I was unable to find God again. All the monastery visits, all the work, had it been for nothing? Being neither Catholic or male, I couldn't live within the walls of any monastery as a permanent resident and I knew I wasn't called to a full time life in that setting anyway. I couldn't be a monk. I was too loud to be a nun and again, the Catholic thing.

I longed to live as a monastic and I felt the pull to that lifestyle at times in ways that brought physically pain. My heart ached for the connection and it was around that time I started referring to my spiritual life as being homesick for Heaven. But, building my own chapel in my backyard and staying there for hours on end praying and chanting by candlelight just wasn't going to cut it. The pay was terrible and I really hate spiders. There had to be a way to keep the parts of the monk's lifestyle that made my soul connect to the Almighty and participate in the sacred rhythm possible while living in the real world. I had to be able to sleep at night in my comfy feather bed, have a career that I was also called to, wear modern clothes and beautiful high heels, drink amazing coffee, and still keep the liturgy in the forefront of my heart.

Heavenly King, Comforter, Spirit of Truth,
everywhere present and filling all things,
Treasury of Blessings and Giver of Life,
come and dwell within us,
cleanse us of all stain,
and save our souls, O gracious One.

-The Office of Great Compline

Compline: The final prayer office of the day

I closed the door of my small room and turned the key knowing this would be my last visit for awhile. A touch of sadness washed over me as I realized the khaki pants, comfortable t-shirt and all weather sport sandals were proof that I had come a long way in my monastic journey. I smiled and headed to the lobby to return my key and prepare for home. I passed the front desk where instead of the first monk I'd seen so many years ago, there was a plaque in his honor. I missed him in that moment and the memory of him telling me to listen for the bells. How many bells had beckoned me to prayer in over a decade at various monasteries within several communities? As if on que, the bells rang once calling the community to Compline.

I put my suitcase in the car and walked the few feet to the chapel settling into a back seat and feeling the finality of that moment. I exhaled grateful that God had met me so many times in so many ways in the hours and days I'd spent within the walls. I couldn't help but smile as I watched the monks leave the chapel and the lights go down, a single candle remaining lit. I walked outside and slid down the smooth exterior of the chapel wall like I had so many years before. I had to get going, but I needed this moment. "Thank you God for offering me the gift of yourself here when I couldn't find you anywhere else. Please. Don't leave me now. Help me figure out how to take you with me."

I climbed into my car and smiled at the solid wood crucifix sitting in the seat beside me. I got it less as great spiritual worth, and more as a sweet reminder of that day so long ago when I saw Jesus still on the cross in my room and freaked out. I couldn't help but say out loud, "We've come a long way." I left that day certain that God wasn't just going home with me in that crucifix, he was going home with me in my heart. The comfort in the grace and peace of that moment almost took my breath away. I not only could love him outside the walls like I had inside; I would.

As if I needed further evidence that God was omni-present – a bell rang.

We celebrate the memorial of our
redemption…..

— THE BOOK OF COMMON PRAYER

CHAPTER 8

Communion

The Eucharist is celebrated in different denominations in several ways. Whether the body and blood of Christ is literal or implied, whether the bread is delivered to the pew or at the altar and whether the blood comes in a bottle of grape juice or a pitcher of wine is really not that important. What does matter in the monastery and in the real world is how we approach the table.

Most monastic communities celebrate the Eucharist every day. Limited by the Roman Catholic tradition, only those who profess to be Catholics including the brothers and visitors are welcome to participate. As a baptized woman in love with her Creator, I'm not going to lie, that makes me nuts. But, I respect their way of life, and because they won't let me anyway, I don't partake of the sacred meal during my stay there.

Due to a whole bunch of hurt, some of which I caused myself and some that was imposed upon me, I left the church completely a few years ago. It was not an easy decision. I remember feeling like I couldn't go back in the doors so frustrated with the Protestant tradition, and more so the circumstances that led to me leaving my own church. I was tired. Really tired. Of religion, of superiority of denominations, of free flying judgments around every corner, and the mean spirited gossiping that showed up under the pretense of prayer requests. To be fair, I know this happens in every tradition and I'm certainly not picking on any one in particular. I missed the monastery. I missed the reverence. And I missed that spiritual connection. My soul hurt. "God. Where are you?" Nothing in this life has made me feel more lost and lonely than being without a church family. I like my social life to be connected to the church. I like my people to be those people. I believe any community of faith is seriously called to mourn with those who mourn and rejoice with those who rejoice. In life, in death, in good times and bad, I like being a part of that. I like the connection of worshipping God with like minded people.

I spent the next year visiting every church I could think of. I spent time in almost every denomination. I met some people. I listened to a lot of sermons. I sometimes sat next to people I knew and sometimes not. It made me more sad to leave every Sunday knowing that wasn't where I belonged either. I just wanted to walk into any building anywhere and see a sign on the door void of titles and credentials that said, "We love God. Join us!" That's all I wanted. I needed some people who loved Him and wanted me to love Him with them. I prayed that God would lead me exactly where I needed to be, but as the year wore on I was getting very discouraged. Was it God's will for me to be a spiritual island? Surely not.

Like always, God came to rescue just in time. I had to walk through that year so that when I found Him, really found Him, I would know. Christmas eve two years ago something, or more likely Someone, spoke to me to go to midnight mass at the local Catholic church. It sounded so right, but I had no idea if there even was such a thing or what happened there. I looked up the website and discovered there actually was a service and, much like the desperation I felt before that first trip to the monastery, I decided I would go. Why not? Again I found myself in a position where I would have to go alone, not really wanting to invite my Protestant friends to join me on yet another spiritual adventure. But, I couldn't help but sense that feeling again that this was the way God had orchestrated it. That has rung true over and over again in significant ways and minor events on my journey Home. When God does something big, sometimes He orchestrates it to where He gets all the credit. Because I'll take it if I can find it. But, I tend to be a little more humble when all of me is gone. Where I'm left standing in the middle of a blessed moment knowing there wasn't anything I could have done to make that happen. That's the life of faith. Entrusting what we cannot see, what we cannot fix, and what we can't make possible to the One who can. When we've come to the end of all that we know, we know He's there. And it's enough. And as long as we find ourselves in the human condition living with spiritual eyes, it doesn't have to make sense.

I slipped quietly into the back pew at 11:59 p.m. in the huge Catholic church and bowed my head. Christmas Eve. How I love the story of the nativity. How heaven came down in the moment and whispered through the atmosphere, "Never again will you be without Me. I've come to dwell among you." I couldn't help but think what I think every Christmas. That somewhere in a little stable next to an at capacity inn as the baby took his first breath, a woman leaned out the stone window and whispered to her husband, "Does the world feel different to you tonight?"

The angelic choir was echoing familiar Christmas carols from the front of the church and the air was thick with incense. My soul stepped without invitation into familiar territory and I realized quickly if I closed my eyes I was back at the monastery listening to ancient prayers with a group of people. The spiritual loneliness lifted in that moment of a deep sigh and for the first time in over a year I found God corporately in a way that brought connection. I'd been holding my breath for so long. It was a beautiful service, but leaving there some-how I knew the Catholic church wouldn't be a forever home for me.

Recalling my Christmas Eve encounter with the Divine to a friend the next day who knew what a long year it had been, she casually suggested The Episcopal Church might be worth checking out. If I'd heard of it before that moment, I couldn't remember. I knew nothing, never remembered even seeing one and haphazardly flipped open the phone book deciding to go once to the closest one and then that was it. I was tired of searching. I just couldn't walk into another church one more time where my soul felt empty and my heart lonely. I couldn't do it and I wouldn't do it. But, I promised God I would try one last church and decided to go the first Sunday of January. Exhausted from following a treasure map to nowhere, my

New Year's Resolution was to sink or swim. And I was halfway prepared to sink.

I parked my car that morning and bowed my head, "God. Once more I have no idea what I'm doing or what You're doing and I'm way too tired for it to matter. I know you show up best when I'm at the end of everything I know, so one more time I'm telling you, I trust you with me." That first Sunday in January I rounded the sidewalk and saw a sign suspended from a pole. "The Episcopal Church Welcomes You." They were just words on a metal sign, but somehow I believed them. I stepped into the back door and was enthusiastically greeted by at least six people dressed in long white robes. I looked up and smiled thinking God had a really great sense of humor.

I sat in the pew that morning and felt like I was back at my first visit to the monastery. "I know nothing about this tradition, I don't know what to do and I don't even know how I know, but I am absolutely 100% sure – I am home." My soul took over everything that made sense and all my insecurities and just made a decision not allowing the rest of me to rebel. Period. It was over. The end. It was as if God himself arrived on the scene in that moment announcing that I had waited long enough and I had never been more thankful in my life. I spent several weeks feeling like the new person not knowing when to sit, stand, speak, repeat. I felt a little like a puppy on the first day of obedience school. But, Sunday after Wednesday after Sunday, I caught on and soon was reciting the prayers along with the other people. I started to recognize others and actually began viewing the Peace as a warm encounter instead of a massive invasion of my privacy. People I didn't even know shook my hand and hugged me and it wasn't strange or uncomfortable. I would leave that place, especially in the beginning, feeling loved by a great God and the presence of His people.

And I liked a lot of things about that church, but, what sealed the deal for me was the Eucharist. At first it seemed like a lot of communion. Every time I walked through the door we were partaking in the body and blood our Lord Jesus Christ. It wasn't the once a month plate pass I was used to and I started to wonder if it wasn't a little bit overkill. But, every time I knelt in my pew and recited the confession I fell in love with the Eucharist and how it enabled me to keep short accounts. Knowing I would approach the table of the Lord at least twice a week kept me awake regarding my spiritual shortcomings and flat out sins. It became the central theme of my worship.

"Have mercy upon us, most merciful Father. In your compassion, forgive us our sins. Known and unknown. Things done and left undone. And so uphold us by your

Spirit that we may live and serve you in newness of life to the glory of God the Father. Amen" BCP, 1979

There's something so eternal to then hear the priest declare, "Almighty God have mercy on you, forgive you all your sins through our Lord Jesus Christ, strengthen you in all goodness, and by the power of the Holy Spirit keep you in eternal life. *Amen*"

I like the whole process. I like the all the silver and the glass. I like that every turn of the cloth and distribution of the elements has a meaning and a purpose. I get all caught up in it. Really. I like the preparedness of the liturgy and how it leads us from death into life. I like the confession. I like approaching the altar, kneeling at the rail and reaching my hands across the invisible barrier where God has just been invited to dwell. There's something so humbling about being served the body and the blood individually and focusing on each element in the company of those with whom you are in community. It's beautiful and to this day, almost two years later, I still get chills when the priest declares, "We celebrate the memorial of our redemption."

And I always feel brand new leaving that altar and returning to my pew and kneeling before, as a congregation we pray, "Eternal God, Heavenly Father, you have graciously accepted us as living members of your son our savior Jesus Christ. And you have fed us with spiritual food in the sacrament of his body and blood. Send us now into the world in peace to love and serve you, with gladness and singleness of heart, through Christ our Lord, Amen."

Amen.

A Collect for Guidance

O heavenly Father, in whom we
live and move and have our being:
We humbly pray thee so to guide
and govern us by thy Holy Spirit,
that in all the cares and occupations
of our life we may not forget thee,
but may remember that we are ever
walking in thy sight; through
Jesus Christ our Lord. Amen.

— BCP, 1979

CHAPTER 9

Present Day Practices

Running late for a seminar on contemplative prayer, I screeched into the parking lot on two wheels. I am not one to compare monasteries. I know that each one is called to be exactly as they are, but this one was by far my favorite. I had started this monastic journey at this place, with those people and they held a special place in my heart. The vast expanse of land called to my soul to come closer, soak in the beauty, and find God in the moment. I had experienced the peace of God in that place unlike anywhere else, and that was in part due to an incredible lack of distractions. It's as close to Heaven on Earth I can imagine this side of eternity. One half step onto the grounds and I remember that God is love, and he loves me.

Grabbing my purse and jumping out of my car, I was surprised to find myself behind the cable guy walking slowly up the ancient stairway. Unsure about him still being in uniform, I convinced myself that we were both there for the same reason. Who doesn't need more prayer? We reached the top of the stairs and he looked around uncomfortably. I pointed toward the office when he looked at me completely lost and he smiled. We reached the desk at the same time and having been instantly sucked into the atmosphere of hospitality, I invited him to go ahead of me. The woman working the office hung up the phone as I checked my watch over and over again knowing I was late. Really late. I only halfway heard him say, "Yes, I'm here to fix the wi-fi."

"I'm sorry, what?" I said mostly to myself. My head jerked toward the conversation in a way that suggested this was none of my business, but I just couldn't help myself. My mind began to race out of control wondering why they had wi-fi at a monastery anyway and secretly why I couldn't use it when we had to go to bed before the sun. She pointed to another office as he picked up his tools. All I could think about was the monks kicked back at night in the lounge watching football on demand and checking their e-mail while downloading the latest episode of Downton Abbey.

I wouldn't claim to know what happens in the privacy of a monastery away from retreat visitors and in the free time of the monks. They live a tight schedule every single day of their lives, but I like to think they get a break on holidays or, more likely, holy days. Do they ever get to chill out with some mindless television? Do they ever leave their Gregorian chant music behind for some upbeat dance tunes? Do they sometimes throw all caution to the wind and stay up until midnight? I don't know. Maybe.

In a world that's ever changing, it's easy to assume that a monastery would be influenced to some extent by the pressures and patterns of life outside the walls. I know a few monks who blog and several monasteries are active on other forms of social media. Most of what I've witnessed has a ministry focus with the intention of bringing people closer to the heart of God. And they are successful. So, while wi-fi may bump up monasteries into this century, in reality, the ancient practices that have maintained these sacred spaces for centuries still remain.

And it's easy to think sitting in a pew at Vespers that these practices could easily be transferred into a busy life with work, family, and other responsibilities all vying for a spot in a limited time frame. It takes work to be a monastic outside of the monastery and more importantly, it takes intention. Worldly everything will attempt to take the place of our spiritual lives especially if we sit back and let it. How many times do we enter into a season of reading the whole bible, memorizing great amounts of scripture, or vowing to pray for thirty minutes every single day only to end up failing miserably and more spiritually discouraged than when we began? It doesn't work, and even when it does, it doesn't last. But, incorporating these practices is not impossible, especially when our hearts are crying out for more.

Sacred space

I'm a firm believer that some of the best prayers happen in the kitchen washing dishes, the car on the way to the store or any five minutes that can be found within the space of the day. They're not planned, written, or rehearsed. They are spontaneous utterances to an ever present, always listening God who longs to connect to His children at any time in any way. The prayers within the liturgy have great value and such an important place, but so do the prayers of "God, help me," that escape from the heart of one desperate for reassurance and comfort. And obviously God hears all prayers at all times.

But just as we find God within the walls of a church building or the halls of a monastery, at times God can be found easier when we have a specific place set aside as sacred. I would never presume to know what will work best for you, but by offering some suggestions, it may provide a starting point. Depending on your level of sensory influence, some may be relevant and others not. The important thing is that what you set in place as a sacred space to connect with the Almighty works for you and enhances and encourages a growing faith.

The space can be as complex as an entire room inside or outside the home or a small chair in the corner of a quiet room. I have friends who use a simple yoga mat on the back porch or a small meditation pillow in the living room near a window that allows the sun to shine through in the morning. Others have set aside a room in their home. Still others take the scripture to go into your closet and pray quite seriously. Circumstances and space will influence what is possible, but with a little creativity, it can be done.

Invoking the senses

For some, smells, bells and whistles do not enhance a spiritual life in any way. And if that's the case, avoid most of the high churches. But, for some, the aspects that engage the senses draw people easier into the spiritual mindset and closer to the heart of God. Through a life of faith, the spiritual toolbox may be filled with different things, in multiple places, with various communities. We learn that finding God where He can be found is always possible, but may not always be the same way.

Personally, I have an entire room in my home set aside for spiritual practices. It's the only way I can function as a modern day monastic. In some seasons I don't spend any time in there and others I spend hours a day. I don't have a check off sheet where I spend thirty minutes a day praying, thinking, reading, etc. I spend time in there when God calls me in there, when I need a quiet moment or a break from an overthinking brain often stuck on repeat. For me, I find God most easily when I can get out of the way. And to do that, I have to connect myself to Him. I choose to do that by leaving a cd on repeat of Gregorian chant music on repeat. It is covered up in candles and incense. My favorite books are in there with giant pillows and soft blankets. My yoga mat and other supplies are in the corner because it's there I practice moving meditation. It's sacred space and I keep it as such.

In today's world there's no need to seek out distractions. They are everywhere. It's important that the space we find to connect with God, stays sanctified. It stays holy. It becomes our own personal arc of the covenant where God lives. I leave everything from my cell phone to my flip flops outside of this room. I only let people in there who are encouraging and supportive of my spiritual walk. I don't allow stress in that space.

There doesn't have to be a huge space to make the sacred fill the ordinary. For some it's an altar. For others, it's a chair or a mat or a corner or a closet. Be intentional to make the space meaningful and it will be sufficient. And even more the surroundings where you find yourself, you'll be surprised how God shows up when we ask.

It is much easier to die like Jesus
if you have lived like
Him for a lifetime.

— MAX LUCADO

Chapter 10

Company at the end

If I wasn't in love with the monastic life before, I certainly was a few years ago when I had the rare opportunity to attend a burial for one of the brothers. Looking around the monastery grounds, it doesn't take long to realize several of the monks, though spiritually strong, are weakening daily in their physical strength. They arrive at prayer several minutes after the younger monks and they are slower to stand. But, they still stand. They don't bow as low as they once may have, but they still bow. And I wondered what it looked like for a community so committed to one another in life, to see each other Home.

As a society, we tend to cover up death and with good reason. No one wants to focus on how a beautiful and well lived life reaches its conclusion. We want to ignore the tragedy or disease that takes one fully alive one minute and lifeless the next. It makes us uncomfortable to experience and participate in what we can't fully understand. There's no one who has died recently to compare notes with. We can only ask questions to those in the same condition and that's a little discouraging. We use hand sanitizer to avoid the common cold and then chastise ourselves when we can't sit with the suffering and comfort the declining. Some are better at coping than others. And although our love for each other is great, it's hard to bear witness to the end due to our own grief and the stark reminders of our own mortality.

Death is absolutely not feared within the monastic walls, but viewed as a natural progression from this life to the next. Preparing for death is part of everyday life. It is the expected and often times welcome result of a life lived in preparation for a glorious reunion with their Creator. Most monasteries have their own infirmary that is able to care for declining or temporarily ill brothers. If further care or surgery is required, outside hospitalization is arranged, but the monk often is returned to the monastery as soon as possible to be under the care of the brothers for healing and recovery.

A monk expected to die soon within the abbey is anointed by the abbot and the other brothers are notified immediately. Whenever possible, a monk that has been hospitalized is returned to the monastery to die at home. The abbey bell is rung and the brothers gather in the room or hallway to pray prayers and psalms together in unison. They wait. They show up at the moment their brother is most vulnerable, perhaps suffering and on a journey he will take alone, and offer the gift of their presence for as long as it takes.

Embalming only occurs when the funeral mass has to be postponed for reasons including waiting on family to arrive or final arrangements to be made. This is becoming the exception as many monasteries are creating natural burial settings for anyone who is interested. All monks are buried today without caskets. In fact, Thomas Merton was the last monk every buried in a casket at the Abbey of Gethsemani. Embalming, when necessary, is done outside of the monastery at a local funeral home who is typically contracted with the abbey and then the body is brought back for burial. The entire community, everyone, gathers to receive the body when it is returned, a united front welcoming the physical shell of their friend back home.

Following a natural death within the abbey, the body is washed and clothed in a clean habit by the brothers.

Generally this is the only preparation needed as burial occurs within 24-48 hours. Once the body has been prepared, a brief ceremony of prayers is held and then the Abbot blesses the body that has been placed on a bier or in an open pine box in front of the abbey church's altar. It is an incredibly simple set up. There are no flowers or video loops of the monk's life. There is no covering the body either. Death is embraced as the loved one is remembered. Monks then take turns day and night keeping prayerful watch beside the body until the time of the funeral. From the time their brother's soul departs the earth, he is never left alone for a minute until he is committed to God at his funeral mass. They take turns standing watch by candlelight all night long praying, reciting psalms, and singing. The night I was there I could see the shadow of the monk standing near the bier and I couldn't help but think of that presence saying, "I've loved you in life serving Christ together day by day. And I will stay with you all the way home." And maybe that's what we're all called to do in life anyway.

During the funeral mass, a monk carrying the processional cross leads community into the church for the service. The Abbot clothed in white vestments symbolizing the resurrection of Christ performs the ceremony and at the end of Mass he blesses the body with incense and sprinkles it with holy water. The community in unison sings "And I will raise him up." Then the procession led by 6 monks begins and the body is carried by them from the church to the graveyard almost always on site of the monastery. The Paschal candle is lit to guide them as a constant reminder of the promised resurrection. During the final procession the bells are rung at solemn intervals until all of the brothers arrive at the gravesite. It is respectfully quiet.

Four straps are laid across the grave dug earlier that day by the hands of the brothers. The deceased monk is laid gently on the straps. At the head of grave, the abbot stands and prays blessing the body and the grave with holy water and incense. A clean, white cloth is placed carefully over the body, the first time it is actually covered, as it is lowered into the ground. The community together sings Psalm 138 and the straps are pulled back when the body reaches the bottom. The Abbot throws the first handfuls of dirt onto the body as the brothers pick up shovels and take turns filling the grave. In recent days everyone in attendance is welcome to participate in the ritual, especially the monk's family and friends. All are invited by the Abbot to pray the Lord's Prayer before the burial ends and they again sing "And I will raise him up." When the song ends, so does the burial. Relatives and friends may gather for refreshments and coffee, but for the monks, it's back to life as usual. Work and reading and prayer. There is no period allotted for mourning. They do not spend the next two hours sitting around and remembering their friend. They knew him. They trust their faith. They are confident that even as they've placed their friend and brother into the ground, he will rise again.

I understood and so appreciated their mindset with death, but it did seem a bit abrupt to one who likes to discuss and process everything over and over again. In that casket was more than another body, this was one who had literally been an essential part of every moment of the life of the abbey for possibly decades. They ate together, worked together, and worshiped together multiple times a day for years. Was there allowed no grief? Could they not mourn? Faith aside, it hurts to be left behind and the soul aches for what has been taken. I don't care who you are.

I got the opportunity to ask those questions early the next morning. Understand that part of the obligation to be cloistered is the monks are separate, from even the retreat visitors. Just because they willingly open their home up to those seeking God doesn't mean they are necessarily involved in the process of spiritual renewal. But, at some monasteries you can establish an appointment with a monk who is trained in spiritual guidance to discuss an issue or seek assistance finding the path to God again. It's not a bad idea to schedule an appointment especially on the first visits. Often they can suggest readings or scriptures that are valuable to your process. And sometimes it's nice for someone specific to know you're lost and not sure how to get home. Whether they can answer your specific questions or not, company is good and feeling like you're not journeying alone is imperative to growth.

As I walked across the burial grounds to get to the chapel the next morning, the memories of the service the day before were as fresh as the overturned dirt making a simple mound on the land. I paused and crossed my arms remembering that whether we are dropped into the ground in only a simple cloth, or serenaded out of this life with lavish fanfare and the most expensive caskets with thousand dollar flower arrangements, the soul still reaches the same ending, or as it is, the beginning.

I strolled in the back door of the chapel where I was supposed to meet Father Matthew that morning. He was already waiting comfortably seated in the back row when I sat down next to him. You would think they would start the conversation to make you feel more comfortable, but I can tell you, they rarely do. Since he was scheduled and stuck with me for the next hour anyway, I decided we might as well talk about what I wanted to. I'm not sure that's always how it works, but that tends to be my pattern of spiritual growth. If I don't know, I ask. If I don't understand it, I don't do it. And I want to know what God looks like, feels like, and how He shows up in your life way more than what church door you enter every Sunday morning. So, that day I was sitting next to a Catholic monk cloistered in a monastery, but for all the reasons that mattered, he had the answers I needed.

"Can we talk about the funeral service yesterday?" I asked glancing in his direction.

"Mass," he answered softly.

"What?" I asked.

"Mass," he repeated patiently. "It's called a funeral mass."

"Uh, okay, whatever it's called, can we talk about that?" I asked a little too quickly.

He smiled and folded his hands as he leaned back in the wooden pew. "Of course, dear." Again it struck me that he wasn't really frustrated by me even though I was probably a touch too animated for that setting and conversation. He was present with me, patient, with the goal of leading me closer to Christ always. Sure, it was part of his job to meet with me that hour, but I got the feeling he wanted to help me find God in that moment even more than I did. It was so comfortable.

I remembered the day before how the brothers had buried their friend and returned to business as usual as I asked him quite seriously, "Don't you miss him? Aren't you sad? How do you just go back to doing what you always do knowing you'll never see him again? It's weird." Sometimes my mouth gets ahead of my brain, but I'm sure he had already figured that out. He looked straight ahead of us at a huge gold cross shimmering in the morning sun and hanging from the highest point of the chapel. I followed his gaze as he traced the cross on the prayer book in his lap with an arthritic finger.

"I'm so, so sad," he said finally, his eyes starting to water. I wasn't sure what to do, so I waited. I'm not sure it's the norm for monks to open up to visitors in such a vulnerable way, but I felt grateful he had that day. "I'm so sad," he repeated carefully. "And I'm not going to say I'm so happy because right now I'm really not and I like to be truthful." That didn't surprise me that honesty was a big priority there. I nodded.

Again he traced the prayer book with his finger, tapped it twice and pointed straight ahead at the hanging cross. "But," he began slowly taking a deep breath, "I am with him already because that part of me that is eternal is not here. My heart is already there." He closed his fist still in the air as if willing himself to believe truth over emotions, and eternity over mortality. He lowered his hand and his gaze slowly back to his tattered prayer book with the loose pages and paused. "And I will see him again, face to face one glorious day. Not now, but not soon enough. It's my calling today to live well until I can go home. Really home. And that, my dear, is your calling, too."

He took a deep breath and settled back into his own thoughts while wiping a tear from his eye. I've never had more respect in my life for another person's perspective or journey. I settled back too and fixed my gaze again on the large cross. We were separated by at least forty years and our lives differed greatly, but our purposes were one. I stayed for a few moments comfortable in the silence and then slowly stood up to leave. He didn't say anything more because there wasn't more to say. But as I opened the back door of the chapel to return to the grounds, I looked at him lost in a gaze that far exceeded earthly eyes. I prayed for him, for his heart, and for his life. And I couldn't help but think that in those moments he had walked me one step closer to Home.

Eternal rest grant unto him, O Lord, and let your perpetual light shine upon him. May the souls of all the faithful departed, through the mercy of God, rest in peace. Amen.

The Kingdom of God is within you.

— LUKE 17:21

EPILOGUE

Closer to Home

Honestly I wasn't paying much attention in church that Wednesday night as the music began signaling the time to celebrate the Eucharist. Running through my head on that hectic day was the errands I needed to finish once church was over and the busy schedule I would have tomorrow. I stood up from my pew looking at my watch and almost ran right into the woman in front of me.

Thankfully, I collected myself before face planting into her paisley sweater. She turned around gently and smiled hopefully unaware that I had just about taken her out. I smiled, too. She had perfect hair ruffled only slightly by the clear oxygen tubing tucked behind her ear.

She made her way to the altar slowly, intentionally and I stayed quietly behind her wanting to see this moment from her vantage point. She had to be at least 85 years old. I wondered how many times in almost nine decades had she walked this path to the table of the Lord.

We knelt side by side at the altar, a half century apart in age, but common in purpose. I honestly do get the seriousness of partaking of the holy sacrament, but in spite of myself, I'm always onto the next thing. I don't savor very many moments and more often than not find myself thinking, "Bread-body, blood-wine, amen, go." But, I didn't that day.

I tried not to stare, but I'm certain I did. "The Body of Christ." She received it into her arthritic hand like she was unworthy to touch the Hope Diamond. She carefully pulled the delicate wafer to her chest and whispered, "Thank you." The one serving communion nodded, but we both knew she wasn't thanking him.

"The Blood of Christ." Her hand shook as she sipped from the silver chalice and a tear fell to the floor beside her. She closed her eyes and the most reverent smile I'd ever seen appeared on her face. I couldn't help but wonder if she was seeing things reserved for those who are closer to Home.

Mesmerized by her reverence, I realized I was still holding my communion and the person serving was patiently waiting for me. I quickly consumed the body and blood and then helped her stand and return to her pew. I willed that the same representation of the crucifixion I had received would soak into the core of my being and change my life like it had hers. I'm not sure I've approached the table of the Lord in the same way since that day.

I haven't been to a monastery since the day I was confirmed into the Episcopal Church. That need for liturgical connection seems to be met locally these days as I worship the One I love with those who love Him in the same way. My heart is still drawn to the ancient words and phrases that people have prayed for centuries and still echo in the halls of monasteries and churches around the world. It helps me to feel like I'm a part of something far greater than myself that will long outlast my earthly existence. But, equally, I want to be part of what God is up to today in my life, in the lives of those around me, and in the world. I want to be there with Him, but until it's my time, I want to be here with Him.

And I will go to monasteries again; the ones that forever have a piece of my heart, and ones I've yet to discover. It's possible I won't find myself within those walls as frequently now that the liturgical tradition is a daily part of my life. But, I'll still go. There's something about physically being there that is so profound you'll really have to experience it for yourself one day. When I hit a spiritual rough patch or an intersection of confusion, my soul begs to be there.

I still participate in monastic practices in my own life with prayer, meditation, lectio divina and contemplative moments, almost every day. I started a journey at a monastery to find God. And I did. I consumed his very presence within those walls and let Him change me. And He's still changing me every single day from outside the walls. His presence was with me then and still is. I often kneel in the room I have set apart for prayer in my own home, close my eyes and picture that huge cross, high ceilings, hard pews and peaceful benches. I remember the words the monks have spoken, and not spoken, into my life and gratitude fills my soul. They prayed for me when I couldn't. They came alongside my journey. They let me stay at their house and worship their God until I remembered it was my God, too. They believed for me when I couldn't always leading me to Christ. You really can't properly thank people for things of that magnitude.

I asked a monk one time why he did what he did. Why he lived in a monastic setting and signed on to something so extreme. And how he helped desperate people every single day find the God he already knew so well. He paused for a moment, of course, before he answered me.

"By the time you're 30, you begin to suspect there's more than this," Father Matthew said. "By the time you're 40, you know it. There's something beyond the obvious. That's not just a superior kind of people who have that insight. Everybody does. They just forget it. We help them to remember."

— THANKS BE TO GOD.

Made in United States
Troutdale, OR
06/30/2025

32527027R00066